MARTIAL MUSIC

MARTIAL MUSIC

GEORGE AMABILE

Clarise Foster, Editor

Signature
EDITIONS

Cover design by Doowah Design.
Cover image: El Tres de Mayo, by Francisco de Goya.
Photo of George Amabile by Annette Willborn.

This book was printed on Ancient Forest Friendly paper.
Printed and bound in Canada by Hignell Book Printing Inc.

Acknowledgments
Some of these poems first appeared in *A/Cross Sections: New Manitoba Writing, Borderlines* (Wales, UK), *Botteghe Oscure, Contemporary Verse II, Conceit Magazine, Crossing Lines, Hungry Hill* (Ireland), *Other Voices, Our Times, Prairie Fire, The New Yorker, Urban Graffiti 11* and *Vintage 92* (Sono Nis Press). "A Disappearance" (with the title "Diminuendo") was awarded third prize in the Petra Kenney International Poetry Competition for 2005. I would like to thank the Canada Council and the Manitoba Arts Council for grants, without which most of these poems may not have been written. I am also grateful to James Scully, who reads my unruly drafts and steers them home.

We acknowledge the support of The Canada Council for the Arts and the Manitoba Arts Council for our publishing program.

Library and Archives Canada Cataloguing in Publication

Amabile, George, 1936–, author
Martial Music / George Amabile.

Poems.
ISBN 978-1-927426-82-1 (paperback)

I. War and society—Poetry. I Title.

PS8551.M32M37 2016 C811'.54 C2016-901569-6

Signature Editions
P.O. Box 206, RPO Corydon, Winnipeg, Manitoba, R3M 3S7
www.signature-editions.com

For my son Evan,
who brings me news of the world

Contents

The fiendlike skill we display in the invention of all manner of death-dealing engines, the vindictiveness with which we carry on our wars, and the misery and desolation that follow in their train, are enough of themselves to distinguish the white civilised man as the most ferocious animal on the face of the earth.

Herman Melville
Typee, 1846

Now days are dragon-ridden, the nightmare
Rides upon sleep: a drunken soldiery
Can leave the mother, murdered at her door,
To crawl in her blood, and go scot-free;
The night can sweat with terror as before
We pieced our thought into philosophy,
And planned to bring the world under a rule,
Who are but weasels fighting in a hole…

William Butler Yeats
"Nineteen Hundred and Nineteen"

IN MEMORIAM

It's up
like a mortar trailing sparks
                                        out of sight.
Pock.
        Over a sea change
of *oohs* and *aahs,*
chalky pink & green
feathers unfold
a voodoo headdress in bright light.

For nearly an hour
there are sizzlers, pinwheels,
lazy stardust
                fallouts
like a Disney film
intro, and the shock
puffs of simple
                    flak,
                        building
toward the climax, punch line, pay-off, denouement:

at the center
of the darkened stadium
Old Glory hisses and glares,
drools liquid fire into the grass
and comes apart, slowly,
like a skin disease under make-up.

The ashes keep flickering
in gridwork that looks like the street plan
of a city that has been burning for thousands of years.

BRICK

Same and not the same, all these
frail-edged tenants of sledge
loads, shaped to stay where a slick
parge sets them, in tight

topple-proof walls or a stout
fence, destined forever to be
what they are, nothing
else, though they also display

attributes we admire:
he, or she, is a brick,
we say, a mute
replaceable unit that keeps

the team keen, and locked
on target, a solid base
we know how to multiply
and make use of. Numberless,

nearly invisible pockets
of air make them easy
to break anywhere,
and ready to soak up

coat after coat of public
whitewash. Whole
cities, whole civilizations:
nothing left but ruins we pay

to see centuries later. Standing
before the walls of Hadrian
or Diocletian, we are struck
speechless by fortress power

stripped of its marble, revealed
as common clay dried in the sun,
drab, colossal, the work of so many
dead hands without names.

STICKS AND STONES

The Museo has devoted an entire floor
to the history of weapons. Out in the light
the columned facade of a temple
sacred once to Diana is pocked
with bullet-holes from The Great War.

News Stands are still selling posters:
Benito's fat lips and thick neck, Adolf's
cowlick and rat's eyes and clipped moustache,
the first white rush at Los Alamos. . .

And there are books, more every day, explaining
with restrained awe and subdued satisfaction,
that we've always had the know-how to develop
improved ways and means, more compelling reasons,
to kill: humans, animals, insects, weeds.

HISTORY LESSON

We stand before a flight of stone
stairs that lead up, and up
to nothing but a cool breeze

above the disappeared
villa of a Magistrate
who marketed fair-skinned boys,

Greek tutors, Abyssinian virgins
and made a fortune serious enough
to buy his place in the Senate.

Years go by. Then, unwilling
to listen or unable to read
the signs, he finds himself

on the wrong side of the room,
red-faced and swearing in a striped
tunic, wheedling, glancing once

or twice at that rude gang
of upstarts, but forcing his attentions
back to business just in time

to miss the way blood sprays
a patch of sunlit marble
but echoing shouts that twist

in the dome wrestle him
back and he remembers
legends: an Egyptian King,

the world's longest river, turned
suddenly red, a burst of hail
and fire, insect wings choking the sun.

REMNANTS OF EMPIRE

1

Fountains glisten and sing
                                        in the wind
that blows as it did for Hadrian once
at his Tivoli Villa. A water jet
struggles to keep its willowy shape in a storm
of rainbows. I see what he
might have seen — Aphrodite, crowned
with foam, deep in the mind.

The stone women of Karyai
seem to withstand the same wind
that sweeps the reflective pool to chipped marble,
but the soaked folds of their garments
are pressed flat against thighs
and nipples by imagined weather,
by desire eased out of thought
and found again at the powdering tip
of a chisel. It blows
where he stood, where I stand now,
has blown for thousands of years
in the flesh, between water and stone.

2

Night. I walk the streets
of Rome for hours, climb
stone stairs toward a window
that soaks clotheslines
and laundry with kitchen light,
cross a *piazza*, follow a crumbling wall
back toward the heart
of the city and come out, blinking,
into the glare
of *The American Bar.*

Tonight, the place is almost
empty. A woman
sits by herself. Light
from the shape-shifting flame
of a candle plays
over her face and makes her look
like a reflection on water.

I watch a current of blue
smoke speed up and slip
through an air vent's crusted grid
like the ghost of a river
lost in a city of dust.

SALEM REVISITED

As a tourist I'm drawn
to the small but famous church
where the pulpit is a dead ringer
for the prow of a *Pequod* harpoon boat
heaving over the ranked pews.

Outside, in the dawn's early light,
league after league of nothing
over the sea, and an Autumn breeze
that scatters the sun on Proctor's Pond
to echos of distant fire
under the shrill cries
of gulls.
            Shouldn't there be
voices edged with a sting
of regret, or the blown glass sculpture
of a scream?
                    Perhaps,
but there is only this
thin whisk of wind in the maples
and sycamores, where pinpoints of rot
eat the red and yellow leaves, leaving
black holes in a roar of glory.

SIMULACRUM

What I've always thought of
                                        as Freedom
may just be a way
                            of wasting more and more time:
week-long tours
of local shops, bars, museums,
afternoons in the sun, evenings
on the terrace, watching
harbor lights and stars. Hours.
Learning to blow smoke rings,
memorizing the names
                                  of tropical birds,
trying to choose
                            between Pineapple-Orange
and Five Alive.

                              Time goes by,
like spilt milk, like water
under the bridge.
                              War
breaks out, a TV sports event, interrupted
by high-tech rumours and lies. The markets
wobble, rally, dip and slide
sideways. The graphs are jagged
cordilleras of profit and loss. A record-
breaking baseball great (retired)
goes on trial for palming
a woman's breast in a club.
There's another earthquake, a flood; a volcano
smokes and glows all night. The magazines
feature questionnaires: Is it really
Love? Are you wearing the right clothes
for your ethnic profile and blood
type?   Do you suffer

from invisible stress, boredom, whimsical
irrelevance or an undiagnosed loss
of momentum? Pills. Potions. Regimens.
An assembly line of triggers and lures
becomes the world in which we are free
to drift, to go with the flow, to follow
trends and gurus and presidents, the path
of least intelligence, but no matter
how quickly we change brands,
and partners, the cutting edge
of day will correct our dreams.

OLIVES AND WELLS

the commerce between them
is human. centuries
go by. branches twist
in the wind, grow
more and more
silvery, like other trees
in moonlight, but today
dawn brings the giant
Caterpillars, claws
dig in, lifting
                    roots, toppling
leaf-tip and wind-sway
from their place in the sky,
and miles away, a back-hoe
stuffs a green mouth with sand.

NIGHT WINDOW

A spray of white
stars and a sickle
moon on the blue

shade, lit
from inside. I sit
in the car, listening

to *news*: of the war, shells
blowing up taxis and hospitals, news:
of a sniper loose on the freeway,

suicide bombers, guns
in the schools. He's
asleep in his crib,

no blanket, his legs tucked
under his chest, shadow bars
like prison stripes across

his back. I remember
rocking him in the soft light
before nightfall, the comfort

of his weight, and the way
he takes my glasses
off, carefully

folds them
and hands them
back, like a cancelled weapon.

TWILIGHT / DAYLIGHT

Birds collect on the telephone wires
like blots in a child's drawing
as bronze bells pulse through the valley
dusk, and seem to ignite
pinpoints of pale fire
that drift in clusters and broken chains
toward the darkening paths
between the courthouse and the church.

Thousands of faces, each one
in the light of its own wavering flame,
stare up at the white cage
of the bandstand. There will be
no brassy fanfares tonight, no stars
or stripes, there will only be voices
we've heard before, not often
enough or in the right
places.

          On the other side
of the world, it's morning. Children
play among rubble, broken
houses, torn up trees. A small girl
stops. At her feet, something
she's always wanted, a bright
yellow ball. She stoops
and reaches, becomes, briefly, a flower,
a fountain
                    of fire
                              and blood.

MARTIAL MUSIC

The balance of objectives
against possible outcomes
tips into chaos. What
is supposed
                              to happen
won't but who knows
how the world will change
after these explosions?

Expect what cannot be
predicted but never admit
that wars can be lost
causes. Expect fire
and death. Resistance.
Retaliation. A climate
of increased hostility
in the world we label
"Third," a necessary
note in the classic
steps toward harmony.

But what about the fifth
world, or the seventh,
that indelible blue
signature of universal
misery and pain? It's
coming, it's already in
the score, down the road,
near the end of the song.

FREEDOM'S FRONT LINE

"Nobody wanted to help the young veterans. Employers weren't interested in whether or not you rose to the rank of platoon sergeant at age 19, that you had led men or had just followed bravely into battle, whether you had spilled your own blood and plenty of the enemy's on freedom's front line."

— Dr. H. W. Chalsma

"In my view, war always represents a violation of soldiers' human rights in which the enemy and the soldiers' own armies collaborate more or less equally."

— Jonathan Shay, M.D., Ph.D.

1. Newbie

When they came in from an operation
they weren't friendly at all.
You could see the strain, the mud
all over them, the worn jungle boots.

I didn't know what to do.
I really wanted to talk with those guys,
but they acted as though I wasn't
there, so I just sat and watched.

A few went to the front of the hooch
and started a card game, smoking
marijuana, while the rest went
to their bunks and relaxed. A white
ground soldier, a grunt, got up,
took out his .45 and started to
clean it. I couldn't figure out why
he was standing, then the gun
went off and he shot the black
GI lying next to him. Right through
the head. And nothing happened.
The body was just taken away.

2. Chain of Command

The word was we were going
to be overrun by a large force.
I remember we put up concertina
wire three rolls high out in front
of us, along with the claymores.
And there were 105 howitzers
too, all around the perimeter,
with beehive rounds designed
to take out large groups of personnel,
and the quad 40mm dusters for fire
power. There was concertina wire
behind us too, three rolls, to keep
us from retreating. And I had
the feeling that our lives were just
nothing. Nobody cared if we lived
or died, they just put us out there
because that's all they had, and we
didn't know why, nobody told us
anything. And we were overrun
more than once, for two days,
two hundred dead, killed with flares,
fighting knives, the enemy all drugged up,
fanatical, they wouldn't stop and some
got through the wire and had to be taken
out with bayonets, and pistols. And what
seemed funny about the whole thing, all
of our leaders were in the middle
of the base camp, with men surrounding them
so they wouldn't get hurt because they
were the leaders and our lives didn't count.

3. Quid Pro Quo

The second lieutenants were almost
useless. They were educated, but
had no experience. They would give
orders that got us killed. Then
they would get, you know,
fragged, and it would go on
reports as friendly fire.

4. Kill or Die

We started to go out
on search and destroy.
They would fly us
into villages to burn
and kill, everything,
everyone that was there.

One day, a top sergeant
ordered me to pick up
an M-60 machine gun
and kill all the women
and children. I said
I don't want to do that
I don't have to obey
an order like that, no way.

He held a .45 automatic
to my head and said,
"Fire or I'll kill you,"
and… I did.

5. The Rule

If one person shoots, everyone
shoots. That's the rule.
You might not see
a thing — shoot anyway.
That way, you never know
who killed who. You can say
I didn't kill him. You don't
know who killed him, so
you can say you did, or you didn't.

6. Tools of the Trade

Once we had to shoot
an elephant. It's nothing
I can prove, but I say
we were in Cambodia,
near the Laotian border,
and we came across this
elephant chained to a stake.
We called in and we were
ordered to destroy it. We
started firing with our
M-16's, which are not
elephant rifles, and all
they did was make it scream,
and try to break away,
and it cried, like a baby,
and we kept on firing, because
we wanted to end the noise.

7. First Kill

One night we were out
on an ambush, below the berm
of a graveyard. There was
movement in front of us.
Everyone started shooting,
then it got quiet. A grenade
came down out of the trees
and a friend of mine jumped
on it, but it was a dud. I looked
up and saw a VC hanging
there. He looked at me.
I fired and I dropped him.

All through the night, I
could hear him groaning.
The squad leader said,
"Finish him off, finish him!"
And others were saying
"No, you take him prisoner."
And I said, "No, finish him."
We opened fire and literally
disintegrated his head.
We were all splattered
with brain mass. That
was my first registered
kill. And that morning
when we went out
to take a body count, it
was a shock to see that he
was around twelve years old.

8. These People

Me and my friend Alfie were both qualified
to operate mobile searchlights on a sort of tug.
When the call came for someone to go down
and perform the same duties aboard river boats
we tossed a coin to see who would go,
and he went down to the river. He wasn't there
a couple of weeks when they blew up his boat.
Four sailors and three Marines. There were never
any survivors. When I heard what happened I got
really upset, and I volunteered to go there too.

After that I went back out into the field for a while
with another friend, Eddie. A rocket came down
out of nowhere, and he took third degree burns.
I pulled some of his clothes off, they were still
smoldering. A Corpsman gave him a shot
of morphine. He was crying and I was holding
his hand, more or less, what was left of it,
and he got another shot before he passed out,
or died. It took the chopper quite a while
but they finally came, and picked him up
and I went back to the river.

I trained myself to believe these people,
all Vietnamese, were responsible
for the death of my friends. One time
I put this rifle right in this woman's
mouth, and the kids were freaking out
and I put the bayonet in their faces.
And once, on land patrol, we went
into this village, into this hooch, and
this baby was screaming, and a Marine
picked it up. He said, "Here, catch!"
And I had a fixed bayonet, and the
mother was shrieking and trying to

grab the kid, and the Marine
was throwing it up in the air…
I thought he was going to toss it
to me and I'm glad he didn't because
I don't know if I would have actually
skewered the kid. I just don't know.

9. Touch

In the grey light before dawn
the hootches in the compound
were exploding. This time
they hit us with 122mm rockets.
Then we started getting small
arms fire. And there was this
Canadian. In the Marine Corps!
He didn't even have to be here,
but there he was, right next to me,
in this place that was like a
beach, all sand, and you could smell
the sea, and he made a sort of
"oof" and he fell back and lay there.

By this time it was full daylight.
He looked like he was sleeping
late, his hands folded on his chest.
Ten feet in front of him there was
this… like a toupee, or a wig,
on the ground and as I got closer
I could see that the whole side
of his face and the top of his head
had been taken off, but there was no
blood, it had all sunk in the sand.
I knelt down and I knew that if I
looked back I'd see the inside
of his skull, and I couldn't do that
so I kept looking at the hair of his head
and the side of his face on the ground
and I had to… touch it, and it was
like touching a mask, and this gunnery
Sergeant yelled, "What the hell…?"
and it felt like I had gotten
caught doing something unclean.

10. Thousand-Yard Stare

He died in my arms. There wasn't
a lot I could do. I could look at him
but I couldn't help him. I didn't know
what to tell him. He couldn't talk
but there was that look, like
"What's happening?" a kind of
blank look that just kept looking
at you. He died with his eyes wide.

11. The Cure

I remember us getting picked
off, one at a time, every day, and
picking up body parts. After
we were overrun, we had to go
on a body count, and we got
a bit ambitious — we were posing
them in certain positions, and then
we started taking illumination
grenades and burning their faces
off. That night the wind
shifted, and the whole trench
line started puking. The stink.
Jesus, that smell was enough
to cure anyone of burning
people after you killed them.

12. The 20th of January

That night at about 9:30,
we took a really intense
artillery barrage. All of the officers
were killed immediately, the staff,
the head corpsman, all of them, dead.
A few minutes later, they came up
the hill. The squad between me
and Cecil were killed, and the NV
kept coming — I couldn't shoot
fast enough and they finally jumped
the trench and they were in it
with us about two in the morning.
Chavez had run out of rifle rounds
and was using his pistol to fight them
off, but he ran out of that ammo
too and they were all over him,
with bayonets and we couldn't
get to where he was and this
went on all night, in close, people
were getting killed with two-by-fours,
knives, rocks. I must have thrown
a case of grenades, and I fired that
M-79 shotgun until I couldn't hold it
up anymore and when morning came
there were only twelve of us. We took
eleven prisoners. And sometime
after sunrise, Cecil told the gun team
to my left, "You guys need
to get your asses down in that parapet,
or you're going to get killed."
And they said okay but they didn't
move and a few minutes later an RPG
landed and killed them all, even
the kid, Panelli, it just blew his head
right off, so Cecil took the POW's
down in the trench and we shot them
and cut their heads off too.

13. Everyone Shoots

We had gone up into this village
after a firefight. Sometimes
they fled, as though they were
defeated, but it was just
a trap. There was, ah, an old lady
and a baby. My first sergeant
walked up on her and she
blew his brains out. And when I
realized what had happened, I shot
the woman and I shot the baby too.

14. On-the-Job Training

To this day I don't know
how many kills I have
because I quit counting.
I got to where I enjoyed it.
One day this Papa-san
came out of his hooch,
behind us, and fired
a few rounds that missed,
and by the time we got
turned around, his wife
was out there too,
and his little girl. I
killed all three of them.

15. The Trigger

We began receiving mortars from the village
to the southwest, no, wait, they came
over the village, then there was a lot
of small arms fire from a village
to the other side of the base. An F-4
Phantom jet air strike came in, lighting
a tree line up with napalm. But we were
still receiving rounds from that direction.
There was a lot of confusion, the rounds
that were coming in were from the NVA,
going over the village which was under
attack. I sighted my M-14 on a woman
carrying a child, coming out of the tree line
that was still burning. She wasn't on fire
but she was running from the attack. I knew
she was unarmed, and I followed her
with my rifle sights for a while, a long while
it seemed like, and she got close enough
to where I could see her, and she was holding
the child and running, and I don't know
what it was but I pulled the trigger and she
went down, trying, like the others, to escape
through the burning trees and get to the safety
of our base, and there were more women
and a couple of papa-sans, and the soldiers
around me started opening fire, maybe
because of what I had done, and I stopped
firing, I jumped up and yelled at them
to cease fire, and they started, I can't
explain the sounds, they started to gurgle
and growl, and they looked at me and just
stared and I thought for sure they were going
to kill me because I was spoiling the fun
I had started, and they were joking,
as they fired, about the shooting duck
gallery, and I dove to the ground, and I put
my hands to my head and closed my eyes.

RETREAT

1

Out on the Prairie, where driftwood barns
yaw and sink into wild grass, wind
flutes and *hooos* through the chinks
of abandoned houses. Broken stone
gives the river a voice and steel rusts
behind the Railway Station.
                                        The year turns
toward months of frozen sunlight
and everything I thought of as my life
dissolves into days that are always
changing (like shadows) and always the same.

This is what I wanted,
nothing in mind but the teeth
of a saw, the spray of white
oak dust, geese overhead, a light
sweat that cools as it dries,
and wood smoke in the wind.

2

Behind me the fire crackles and spits.
I sit on a sleeping bag, watching
my shadow-puppet flicker

and glide over frost
on the peeling wall of this upstairs room
that housed an entire family.

In the uncertain light
a ghost appears
and melts with each breath.

Out in the dark, snow
descends on the empty streets, relentless
as volcanic ash. For weeks

I've tried without success to leave
my body, but even that
desire is gone. I forget what I came for.

3

The rotted screen of the sun porch
is scribbled over with vines.

I remember climbing narrow stairs
to the attic, the dry scent,
the chest, the packet of letters,
a tight scrawl mailed
from the war…

Echos
of snow-melt. Deep
in a thicket of whips and shadows,
buds ripen like drops of blood.

4

I wake to a rush of wind in the leaves
and a pulse that flares red across the ceiling.

I pull on some clothes
and stumble downstairs into the night.

We stand around in front of the car.
They've just come out to see if I'm still alive.

The turret light keeps turning, flashing
from handcuffs and guns at their hips.

GETAWAY

1

My only destination now
is elsewhere, a place with more
random light, more dust.

2

Whisky burning in its glass
cage on the bar top;
Cigarette smoke, braiding

and fading away. No one
to talk to though the air
is busy with voices. This

is what I saved myself
and traded my savings for,
a far place, anonymous

as mayhem, built and rebuilt
with broken stone, a town
whose lights are unavailable

for mirror work. Leather
jacket, leather boots. Not the same
animal. I never saw that before.

TEXACO IN ECUADOR

1

Mercedes, *Supermercados* and silk suits
multiply on the streets of Quito,
the Avenidas of Guayaquil.
Tongues of fire lick the night sky.

2

Along the north shore of Rio Napo
the river birds are all dressed up
in black with nowhere to go.
They stagger like drunks, tripping
over their own feet, their eyes
glazed, their wings, their plumage,
fused under the crude sheen
of coal gloss in the sun, then
they collapse and just lie there,
twitching, more and more
weakly until they sink
into the silence like wet clay.

3

Miles downstream,
a boy from the Secoya tribe
strips, dives into the cool water,
swims for a while, then floats
on his stomach, watching
nothing but the green satin
light flow over stones
and when he feels
clean he crawls across
the current, climbs up the bank
and stands, a dripping sandalwood
Ephebe against the jungle
shade, barely a trace
of hair around his genitals,
until darkness shrinks the field
of his vision and he moans, falls
to the grass and the river
takes his breath, his voice
where it will not be heard again.

DEATH SQUAD

Really proud. Trained in the US of A.
No uniforms, but the best weapons.
The best pay too. What we do
is root out every sick cell
of the threat, then erase it.

When agitators choose to hide
among the *peones* and the priests,
or when village elders tell us they know
nothing, we crank the first shell
into the chamber of an AK-47
and send them all to heaven, or to hell.

DEEP IN THE MYTH OF THIS HISTORICAL MOMENT

Pursuit initiatives no longer even approximate
the avidity of those invisible proponents
who pay others to calibrate our tendencies
and limit proximity while they delve and squander
from a privileged enclave of white noise and Kevlar.

Tomorrow there will be more of the same,
affirmations backed by *outre* weapons and soft
rocket fire over a succession of landscapes
Cezanne couldn't mix a palette for. Who cares
how they burn, when violence enhances acquisition.

Brawling rivers and tacit wings are all
gone into a spiral of appetites and the earth itself
blinks and blinks as it turns with the infinite
patience of a sharpening stone and the idea
of perfectible anything at all gets thinner and thinner
till it cuts down, through papyrus dictionaries,
and sails free in the dust no one notices, the dust
of Millennia, mythic attributes and fashions
wrinkling toward disintegration, spun by the same
flash and backlash we carry in our signal storm
but pretend we never heard of. Well, me too.
And like most animals I'd be happy to erase
everything that scares me as it approaches
the limit of what can be known, the event horizon,
the slur where thought murmurs into dream and the night
disappears. Pyramids. Cathedrals. Moon Shots.
Labor intensive betrayals that warp the time line.
We emerge like twisted embryos from the wreckage
of our last mirage, what it means to come home, that race
through the sunlit evergreens, water itself
bashed white by stone-cold energies that defy
contradiction. Where else should we expect to be,
given the choices that have been made for us, thousands
of years and a trillion words ago, while the long legged birds
and the butterflies gutter, then die out one by one.

A GLIMPSE OF PARADISE

Effortlessly we enter the no-man's landing halfway up
the spiral stairs between the first reading and the second
brazen amnesia which absolves us of everything
we haven't thought or done yet, and this is how we go

on without direction, breathing dry-ice fog and celebrating
people we've never met whose faces remind us of nothing
like our own residual compunctions and their lazy flags
as color-blind innuendoes wrap us in comfort plaids and deft
wraiths left over from the wars we dreamed of but never attended.
And whereas the effects of a healthy senescence can no longer be
attributed to slathering or lax attention, its clear they favor the patriotic
assumptions of personal avarice, burgeoning but unable to read
stone-cold warnings between the celebrity posters and high-gloss whisky
ads as thousands rise to their feet and the steel rafters
ring with shouts in the all-weather domes where bodies bang.

This is another indication that we are where we are and nowhere
like it as well. But it's not useful to know these things, so let's
forget them, along with those days of whines and doldrums,
let's remember, instead, the good times, when uniforms ruled,
whacking out the irregulars and launching their batons against
all levity as the assiduous and random alike aligned where nothing
but vapors burned and the hard corps were rinsed clean
by tomorrow's invisible crimes as we watch a now familiar
crisis tumble and smear the global economy with a streak
of lies fueled by webcam abandon and undecided voting
machines that spin their gears with small squeaks of denial,
in love with popular quackery and paid-for bad health.

It's true. We're beyond all complaisance now that we've apprised
and weathered the next stage of comeuppance where techni-facts
feed practical stemcells to the largessed and tantamount heredities
we examine only as an adjunct to astonished applause, because
to do otherwise would surely erase festivities at the brass root
and authorize escape clauses in the drift of promiscuous habit.
Batten the ramifications. Erode the crustaceous outcrops
that hinder the unsuccorable and let them join us in our bath
of oiled evasions, knowing that we will never have to regress
further than our already cozened intuitions and dead dreams
have led us, all the way back to a bonfire of incriminating innocence
where we will take ourselves seriously over, and never die.

COMIC BOOKS AND DEAD SOLDIERS

Heros validate a poisonous exuberance with blood
on its hand-maidens and tears in its crocodile profits.
This is a custom, not a law. The Greeks loved it.
But the Romans, ah the Romans, they (and of course
the Japanese, the Persians, the Brits, the Huns)
raised it to the status of a world view, complete
with a stunning avalanche of uniformed and weapon-
savvy slaves, the trained ones, disposable as their arms
and legs, and even this badly named "America"
has given it clumsy wings immune to intelligence
or practical self interest. We are riveted to our place
mats by centralized electrons, across a lapse
of actual fact in fractured inertia while we dream
the dream spun from an irrepressible lust for power
bars and excused absences from the gears that grind
without conscience in the offices where consent
of the governed is manufactured and brain cells
reverberate to flags, anthems, selected history,
and truth is tossed about like a ham, or laced
like a punch at a dance and we are fed the offspring
of ancient rhetorics that still squirm enough to turn
our heads. Is it comforting to realize, before we die,
that back in the days of grandeur and glory, the same
rust came down from above to close the frontiers?

A CASE FOR PRE-EMPTIVE WAR

Danger.

They're trying to build hideous weapons
that will destroy us. We can believe this
because we know for a fact that they are *not*
us. And though they look like they might be
human it doesn't mean they are. Notice
how the sounds they make make nonsense
of our beloved syllables. And their scalps
are covered with sleek black pelts instead
of hair. Even their clothes are only scruffy
attempts at worsteds or twills. They *all*
wear scarves and loose dresses, men,
women, girls and boys. What does that
tell you?   Up close, their breath is a
miasma of stinks and fumes. Breath
of the dragon, breath of unspeakable
acts. We have a Sacred Trust, we must
attack, destroy them first, protect
our Civilized Realm from such
savagery. No matter how much
it costs or how long it takes.

COUNTER INTELLIGENCE

Kept naked in a cell
the size of a kennel cage
that is never cleaned, fed
one bowl of gruel a day.
And every day her head
fills with the black smell
of the hood that takes her breath
away as her heart races
and her chest heaves in the wet
rush that covers her face
and keeps her locked in a well
of terror still as death.

By the time they drag her out
of the water her lungs burn
with it. They take turns,
slap her awake and shout
insults, questions, threats.
But she's told them everything
she knows, which is nothing.

She feels the cold sweat
collect on her skin; in her ears
that sound like a flat-lined heart
monitor. When they start
to drown her again, she fears
this is it, they're not bluffing.
She'll die, she must think of something
to say that they want to hear.

IMPACT

The khaki Humvee hits a bump
in the blacktop and the back
tires blow off, the rims
scraping sparks as it slews
off the road into sand and those
who are leaving forever
their bombed out homes turn
in the glare and cheer,
their tongues fluttering shrill
falsettos as what they don't have
to fear or hate for a while bursts
into flame and the screams
of ordinary flesh dim to nothing
at all in the crackle and hiss
as black smoke churns
but stays like a tall ruck in the blue
absence of anything anyone
can remember about their lives
before a nest of lies hatched
without eyes and blinded the world.

OUT-TAKES

1

Aluminum coffins
emerge like giant eggs
from the bellies of transport planes.
They are draped with flags and rushed into the night.

2

There are nine Afghanis, aged from five
to fourteen, gathering firewood. They are seen
by helicopters responding to a rocket
attack on their command base.
The children are tracked
down and machine gunned, one
at a time. Petraeus
offers the usual grave,
heartfelt apology.

3

An Army Captain
decapitates a civilian.
He has good reason.
When he raped and murdered
the Afghan's baby
sister, the man attacked
a US Patrol and hacked
an officer to death. He was brought
in, and the rapist Captain
whose detail was assigned to transport
the Afghan to prison,
carried the man's head back
to HQ in a sack. The Captain
was tried and acquitted. The court agreed
with his lawyer's claim that the head
was fair exchange, and was taken in self defence.

4

Sgt. C. G. tosses a live grenade
at an Afghani
he has caught committing the crime
of walking home
alone, after work, after dark.

It explodes, but the man is still
standing, weaving,
his left arm a loose, bloody rag
his eyes wild.

"Wax him!"
the Sgt. screams, at his Corporal,
at his PFC's, "Shoot
that Guy! Kill Him!"
and they do.

5

Three women in black
aba and *hijab* kneel
holding each other
and praying, in whispers,
in the corner, their backs
against the wall, on the dirt
floor of their small house
in a village to the south
of the Capital. Their eyes
are wild, watching
their own fates unfold, next
to their men and four
boys, stretched out
in a row, as though
asleep with their eyes
open who cannot see
shattered windows,
bullet holes in the walls,

in the door, or the stars
and stripes on the sleeves
of soldiers who kneel
to take turns at the girl
who will not scream
but stares as though
she were so far away
they're just another
wild rumour of war.

After they shoot the women
they burn the place down.

One of the men
who watched, did
nothing and told
no one goes on
seeing it, awake
and asleep, for years
until he stands
in front of the bedroom
mirror and eats his gun.

THE HOME FRONT

This is the moment of no
return, again. Voices
                                        escalate. The child
stands with his hands behind him, waiting
for the uneasy silence that will cue his escape
into sleep.
                    Hours later,
no one has won, or lost.

They move away, to different parts
of the house, hoarding
resentments, vowing they will never
speak to each other
or inhabit the same room
again.
            Motives. Beliefs.
Psychosomatic headaches. None
of it matters, they are committed
to splintered door jambs,
shattered glass,
wires ripped from the wall.

And they find reasons to go on
exploding
                    knots of despair,
                                                    releasing
misery that hangs in the air like smoke
of an old war. They cannot agree,
and cannot decide unilaterally
what needs to be changed or why
they have never taken their own lives
seriously. In their hearts, these
episodes always end with the same
word. *Goodbye.* But they
can't say it. They're in love
with this tangled thing they do not want
and cannot walk away from.

THE DARK SIDE

The air is taut with a hint of frosts
to come, but it's hard to believe
we've already reached All Hallows Eve
again, the same paper ghosts

in the windows, and on so many porches
those toothy grins lit from inside —
iconic innocence disguised
as horror, like the small tribe that marches

house to house, dressed up to kill
in Devil mask and Pirate hat
chanting a customary threat,
harmless, but good enough to fill

their plastic Safeway bag with sweets
they'll carry home and stash like *wonder*
-kinder raiders flush with plunder.
In another part of town, where the streets

are deserted and unlit, there are real
screams. A woman is raped, and cut,
left with her mouth taped shut,
her hands and feet bound with steel

wire, half dead in a parking lot.
And that's not the only bad dream
that will release its actual demons
before the teeth of the children rot.

THE SNIPER

doesn't know where
he is. He climbed out
on the fire escape and up to the roof
in his sleep, in his night-

mare, pursued, surrounded,
by shadows and shrieks of wind.
All those he sees on the dawn street,
men, old men, women, kids,

whatever they're wearing, they're still
terrorists, the same
hunched shoulders, the same
fake, going about

their business walk he 'scoped
and tracked and shot as they crossed
dirt tracks in the mountain
villages, more than a thousand

yards away, for eighteen months.
The sun comes up and a blaze
of light burns off the flickering
doubt that haunted his first

kill, and by late afternoon
the body count has mounted
to seventeen, the best day
he's ever had, the last day of his life.

LETHAL WARRIORS

1.

In World War II, they were called Easy Company,
an airborne combat brigade of the Fourth Infantry.
They jumped through the flak-filled skies over Normandy
and stopped German guns on the Causeway from Utah Beach.
In Holland their high risk sorties prevented a breach
of the Allied lines. They became known as The Band
of Brothers. Later, in Vietnam, their Command
took heavy casualties in the bloodiest battle
of the war, the direct assault on Hamburger Hill.

2.

Before Iraq they were kids, too young for a beer
but not for TV. They decided to volunteer
when they saw the ads, the helicopters with guns
blazing, the coolest job in the world, and no one
could disabuse them. At boot camp they were treated
like shit, spit on, cursed, insulted, beat up,
and if they complained, their superiors turned the heat up,
till they were half crazed, confused and disconnected
from their everyday lives then deliberately infected
with the kill virus. What makes the grass grow?
They shout back Blood! Blood! Blood! as they throw
their bodyweight stiff with rage into a thrust
that spears the dummy hadji instead of the bloodlust
-crazed Drill Sergeant they'd shoot if they were sane.
But they're not sane, they're child killers in training.

3.

Months of this, then they're deployed. When they get there
they're told to trust no one. "You're in a war
where every fucking haji would like to shoot you
so it doesn't matter which one you put the boots to."

4.

An eighteen-year-old on top of an armored Humvee
at a traffic control point near Tikrit with a fifty
calibre M-240 thinks Why is this car
coming so fast? And though it's still too far
off to see inside, the butterfly
trigger pours two hundred rounds into the guy
at the wheel, his wife, and their two kids, a boy
who was four and a half, and a girl who was three.

When the unit briefed this to the General
with digital images of the bodies, all
he had to say was, "Well, if those fucking sand
niggers knew how to drive, this shit wouldn't land
in our laps." After that, IED attacks went way
up, from once in a week to three times a day.

5.

Supply convoys kept the war alive.
But they were easy targets; you had to drive
tractor-trailer strings up to a mile
long, loaded with fuel, water, mail,
maintenance parts, sewage and food,
out on the open road with a very crude
line of defense: maybe a Bradley in front,
a Humvee in the middle with a grunt
machine gunner on top, and at the end
another Humvee. We did what we could to defend
the convoy against car bombs. If a motorist got
too close, looked suspicious or tried to pass, he was shot.
Sometimes a bullet riddled car would be left
with its wounded or dead for days before a lift
truck hauled it away. A better defense
was pure speed. You'd be hit with intense
mortar and RPG fire if you could be slowed
or stopped. Sometimes they'd plant a child in the road
but the order was "Never let anything impede
or deter." And, once, we barreled into a kid

who was leading two donkeys across the highway. What we did
to them was ugly, but we'd seen too many good men
get their faces blown off or their chests ripped open.

The biggest threat, by far, is the IED.
You wince at every garbage bag you see
on the shoulder; you avoid medians, you re-train
yourself to drive in the oncoming traffic lane
or up on the sidewalk. It does weird things to your brain.
You ask yourself why the semis are carrying faddy
tee shirts that say things like "Who's your Baghdaddy?"
or sodas and Twinkies, Play Stations and air
conditioners, greeting cards, camping chairs.
And these KBR contractors – it makes you sore
when you find out they're getting paid three or four times more
than the Army pays you. And you think, what for?

6.

A blast that would have killed you two wars ago
doesn't. Body armor. Mortars can blow
you up a dozen times and you're still on your feet,
in the fight, flinching. If you could, you'd get out in a heartbeat.

7.

A lot of old folks and children were selling gas
on the highway and when the Bradleys would pass
they'd all shout and wave at the Americans.
But the soldiers shot holes in their jerry cans
then someone launched a grenade and the roadside exploded
into flame. When interviewed, one of them said,
"It's fun to shoot shit up."

When people were shot,
by accident or otherwise, it was not
looked into most of the time, but they
soon learned to always carry a throwaway,
an AK, or a nine millimeter — like the L. A.

Police — or a radio or a cell phone, or
a shovel: to prove they were caught in the act, terror
by remote control, digging a hole for a bomb.
They'd send HQ the pictures by telecom.

8.

Those fucking camel jockeys are full of tricks.
If you guess wrong, you won't be able to fix it.
Better tried by twelve than carried by six.

An order came down about when to shoot an Iraqi.
He didn't have to threaten or attack me,
he just had to look the wrong way, tough
or insolent or hostile and that was enough.
So the question was no longer up for discussion.
The brass would protect us from legal repercussions
by falsifying reports or planting evidence.
After that we could pretty much kill anyone, with confidence
that the incident would never be investigated.
A lot of unarmed civilians got terminated
and that's one reason Americans are hated
everywhere now. That, and the night raids.

An armed and goggled gang of grunts invades
a quiet neighborhood without warning
at one or three or five o'clock in the morning.
They kick in doors, grab the man of the house,
ram him up against the wall in front of his spouse
and his children, interrogate them all at gunpoint,
dump drawers, spill food from the fridge on the floor and anoint
the place with obscene, anti-Arab graffiti; slash
cushions, smash dishes and windows, trash
furniture, toys, clothes, books. If they found
a locked door they'd blast it with a shotgun round.
And once they used a shaped charge. The sound
was deafening and when the door went down
there was a pregnant woman, blood all around her,
and a six month fetus blown out onto the ground.

9.

We were searching for contraband. If we found a wire,
more than one weapon, or signs of recent gunfire
(expended shells) we would arrest every male
adult, but most of these raids were doomed to fail
because they were based on tips about insurgents
from a source that was known only as "human intelligence."

Our informants were paid and some had ulterior motives.
An Iraqi farmer drives into the base and gives
the address of a crack Iranian Resistance
unit. We check it out. We request assistance,
but there are no interpreters to spare,
so it's a go. We expect they'll have heavy hardware.
We bring grenade launchers, a missile firing Bradley,
and M-240 machine guns on every Humvee.
We rip off the front gate with a chain, then the plan
is to shatter windows and mortar down doors while the van
blares out recorded Arabic commands,
but instead of foreign fighters from Iran
we find a few kids, a woman and an old man.

At other times the informant might have a beef
with a neighbor who looked the wrong way at his wife.
Or it's just business: a lie to counteract
a competitor's better bid on an Army contract.
Sometimes we detained people for the way
they looked or what they were wearing, or else they
had protested their innocence too vociferously,
and we'd spirit them off in the back of a truck or a Humvee
with bags over their heads and their hands tied
with plastic zip-strips behind them. If they tried
to talk, we'd rifle-butt them in the ribs.
No one was told where they were: at Abu Ghraib
or some other internment camp in a damp cell
where the air was thick with an old, stale smell
of blood. They'd be stripped naked, forced to stand
for days on an upended cinder block. The random

glare of a flashlight, heavy metal guitars
that shrieked from a ghetto-blaster at all hours,
and, whenever they felt like it, guards who banged on the bars
with a pipe or a serving tray, kept them awake
for as long as a week. High profile suspects were hung
by the wrists with their toes barely touching the floor, strung
up and beaten till they were strung out, crazy
with pain and lack of sleep and it was easy
to see they'd say whatever you wanted them to say,
but it would be totally worthless; and every day
you kept them, a whole tribe of cousins and friends
would be contacting those who would help them take their revenge.

10.

It's been more than a year since Bush came down from the sky
to declare our mission "accomplished," and victory
is still nowhere to be seen. The body count
for US troops has risen by thirty percent.
And we're getting the worst of it. The numbers are wild:
More than four hundred wounded, sixty-four killed –
twice the average for any Army brigade
in either war. If you thought about it, it made
you feel like you were being picked on. It sucked.
There's no way we can win; this war is fucked.

11.

When Kenneth Eastridge was twelve he killed his best friend.
He pleaded guilty and was given a suspended
sentence because it was ruled an accident.
They were playing with his father's gun and it went
off, on its own, demonstrating the independence
of deadly machines.
Felons are not allowed
into the Armed Forces, but Eastridge found
a recruiting officer who assured him, "Son,
all you need is a second chance to handle a gun."
Over the next eight months, he covered himself

with tattoos. On his arm, the twin lightning bolts of Adolf
Hitler's beloved SS. Around his neck,
BORN TO KILL, READY TO DIE, in black
capitals, wrapping his throat like a clerical collar,
and on his wrists, dotted in red, there were kill
lines, marking the place where he'd slit them if
he were ever captured or had his legs blown off.

12.

In Ramadi, the longer they stayed, the worse it got.
There were power blackouts every day. It was hot,
a hundred and twenty degrees in the shade, and the rubble-
choked streets reeked with sewage. Every bubble
or hump in the heat-waved asphalt looked like a bomb
and insurgents were getting better at head shots. Some
of the men were saying, "This shit is getting old,"
but Eastridge was cool, he loved being a soldier.
"Combat is the biggest rush you can have,"
he said, "It's got nothing to do with being brave.
It's like a religious experience, to be
on a battlefield, to hear the explosions, to see
a person get hit, go down and bleed out.
It makes you realize what it's all about,
life, being truly alive, the fire, the smell
of smoke and burning flesh…" Before he was well
into his first tour, a sniper's bullet
hit the wall so close to his face, grit
peppered his eyes. This happened twice. He laughed
as his luck. A few weeks later the deafening flash
of an anti-tank mine tore off the front end
of his Humvee. He woke up next to a dead friend
a few feet away from the smoking crater, dazed
and bleeding. Medics got him to base camp, gave
him a shot for the pain, made him lie down in bed
while they checked his eyes and bandaged the gash on his head.
He was sent back on patrol an hour later
with cerebral fluid leaking out of his ear.
He sucked it up. Then a truck filled with explosives

careened into his platoon, blew fist-sized holes
in the Sergeant, killed the squad leader and pinned
Jose Barco under the engine that seared off his skin.

13.

Anthony Marquez was a high school athlete.
He co-captained football and won medals at track meets.
When he was assigned to hunt terrorists in the city,
there was no reliable way to confirm their identity,
and though he joked, "It's not as if they had antlers
or uniforms, or tails, or long floppy ears,"
it bothered him. Like others in the Brigade
he spent hours at his computer. The games they played
were shoot-em-ups. One was even based on The Band
of Brothers. They found that having a clearly defined
enemy to destroy helped them unwind.

But the real enemy struck from the shadows. A Lieutenant
was picked off while on street patrol; a friend
got shredded with a car bomb, then another.
He got his hands on a stun gun and used it to rough up
Iraqis on raids though he knew stun guns were banned
and their use was a war crime. There was no reprimand.

His platoon was walking across an open field
when a bullet whistled by his ear and killed
his best friend instantly. They circled and tore
the neighborhood up with grenades and machine-gun fire.

One night, they were hosing a soldier's blood from the Bradley
when they were called out again to downtown Ramadi.
Marquez was riding in the dark, cramped rear
of the vehicle when a blast ripped through the floor.
The engine exploded. Diesel fuel spewed everywhere
and the driver scrambled out, screaming, his clothes in flames.
Marquez and the others climbed through the broken frame
into the street. A second bomb slammed them
to the ground. When he tried to fire, his rifle jammed

and a flurry of bullets came spitting across the dirt.
It took several seconds to realize he was hurt.
He'd been hit four times in the leg. He watched blood spurt
from his femoral artery. He started to arm
his grenade launcher, and that's when he saw the storm
of slugs had come from another Bradley. "They'd seen
the damage, thought it was an attack and machine
gunned the area." Two of the soldiers died
and Marquez was flown back home to Walter Reed
Medical Center. He was still bleary on Morphine
July Fourth when George Bush came to award him
a Purple Heart. His sister hated the war
and her brother's wounds. She refused to see
the president when he arrived, but Anthony
was honored. "It was my job. I blamed nobody."

He was in hospital for three months and endured
seventeen surgeries to keep his shattered
leg. He was being discharged and could have stayed
at the center, but wanted to spend his remaining days
as a soldier with buddies who'd just come back
and would soon return for a second tour in Iraq.

14.

When they got home they were ready to blow off steam.
They had saved thousands of dollars and for the first time
they were old enough to drink in the US of A.
But first they had to debrief. They were told to stay
sober behind the wheel, leave their guns at the post,
be understanding with spouses and loved ones, and most
important, honestly answer a screening test.

Do you have trouble sleeping? Are you depressed?
Did you have friends who were killed? Have you lost interest
in food or sex? Did you shoot anyone? Did you kill
anyone? Were you shot at? Did you see dead civilians?
Were you close to exploding mortars or IED's?
Did you witness any brutality toward detainees?

Did you see dead Americans? Did you see dead babies?

If there were no red flags they'd be let go.
So their answers were always No! No! No!
(And they knew what The Warriors thought about PTSD:
Whiny bitch. Liar. Dirt Bag. Pussy.)

15.

Although Marquez was still in a great deal of pain,
He eventually learned to walk without a cane
but he started having nightmares. He was depressed,
had violent outbursts, and even on his best
days felt empty, crippled, resentful, helpless.

On a visit home, he made his mom put away
his sport trophies and stayed in his room all day
downing old pain pills from the medicine cabinet.
It was clear that he had a serious drug habit
and his mother, who was a peace officer, called
Fort Carson. She told them that her son was about
to explode. They were not impressed. Politely, they stalled.
"We're sorry, ma'am, but we can't do a thing without
a formal request submitted by Private Marquez."
After that, the Sergeant started needling him.
"Hey boy, yer mommy tells me you're a stark
ravin' pussy." By then, his meals were Slim
Jims, Rum, and a handful of Percocets.
He stopped showing up for duty, piled up debts,
and started trading drugs with other vets:
the anti-psychotic Seroquel (quetiapine)
and anxiety pills (clonazepam) for morphine.

He bought three pistols, a riot-style shotgun
and an Army assault rifle like the one
he used in Iraq. He never went anywhere
without one: church, bed, a bar, the Food Fair
or the Mall; even kept one close when he took a shower.
"It makes you less scared and gives you a sense of power."

Eight months later he limped down to the basement
room of a drug dealer, got into an argument
over the price of an ounce of Panama red,
pressed a stun gun against the teenager's head
and fired off a five hundred thousand volt
zap. When the kid fought back, he pulled out his Colt
forty-five, shot him once through the heart and left.

After he was arrested, he said, "I was miffed,
but I would never have done what I did before
the war. It changes you, the blood and gore,
your buddies killed by an enemy that's not there,
then you're burned in a bomb blast. You just don't care
anymore; life is cheap and there's no one you can trust.
If someone grabs you or gives you some shit you just
light 'em up like you did over there where you never got busted."

16.

While Eastridge was waiting in Colorado Springs
between the first and second tour, he did things
that should have kept him there. He began mouthing
off to superiors, or he'd just go south
for weeks at a time, then he got into a drunken
fight with his girlfriend and held a loaded gun
to her head. He was arrested and charged. He went
AWOL. About the same time, his friend,
Gerald Butler, started beating up on his wife.
She never called the police, and for the life
of him he couldn't understand why
he was so angry, but he still thought PTSD
was nothing but a lame, drag-ass excuse.

One night he and some buddies were into the juice.
He said he needed them to do him a favor.
They were all excited but wondered if he'd ever
get away with it. Eastridge drove to a dark
parking lot and that's where Jose Barco
shot Butler through the calf. There was blood

everywhere. His scream woke the neighborhood
and they burned rubber. "It was hilarious,"
Mifflin said, "nothing happened, I swear, he just
got a few days off, and they're gonna send him back
to Iraq anyway." But he did get an open prescription
for Percocets, and that was the other reason
for the leg shot. That Summer, Butler and Nash
were kicked out for snorting cocaine. They should have cashiered
Eastridge too, but when he couldn't be located
the DD stayed on someone's desk, and later
when he showed up and begged to be sent back,
his Commanders decided they needed him in Iraq,
even though regulations forbid deployment when
a soldier has a trial for a felony pending.
He was one of the best gunners in the battalion,
absolutely "surgical" with a machine gun
and utterly fearless. He had the most kills
in his company and had been awarded medals.

17.

In December, when they started their second tour,
The Lethal Warriors were assigned to Al-Doura,
a deadly Baghdad neighborhood where security
had deteriorated. Terrorist bombs killed scores
of civilians. Sunni and Shiite Militias tore
through the houses all night, murdering each other
and tossing the bodies out into the gutter.

First thing in the morning we'd bag them up, guys
with nails in their heads or drill bits in their eyes.
The strain of daily violence was taking its toll.
Discipline failed and some of the men lost control.

We loaded our rifles with hollow points ordered from home.
We had stun guns too. When you hit them, some would foam
at the mouth, or have seizures. We took a few to the bridge,
blindfolded, made them stand on the outer ledge,
interrogated them then pushed them off,

or maybe we'd let them go free if they could cough
up enough dinars. We targeted random cars
and pedestrians as though we were avatars
of disaster. One Sergeant shot a boy on a bike.
A medic rushed over to help and it looked like
he could save him, but Sergeant said, "No, let him bleed out."

The kid wore shorts and knee socks just like a boy scout.

A senior officer shot a man in the head
without provocation, mutilated the dead
body, lashed it to his Humvee hood,
and drove it slowly through all the streets of Baghdad,
loudspeakers blaring a warning in Arabic.

Some of the Sergeants seemed to get a kick
out of removing eyes or brains or toes
and drying them out to take home as mementos.
But there was no time for mental health care in Combat
Outposts. The symptoms could be clear as they come, but
you were given anti-depressants and sent back out
to fight. We were losing a soldier a day to the hospital
or the morgue. We'd come in from a patrol, get a little
sleep, get attacked and go out again, only three
where there used to be five-man teams running the Humvees.

18.

At first, Eastridge was happy to be back
in competition with Bressler to see who could whack
more bad guys. He liked the intensity of it, but after
a few months of snipers and car bombs and other disasters
he couldn't sleep and was always on edge. He
was diagnosed with depression, anxiety,
a serious sleep disorder and PTSD.
They gave him pills and put him back on duty.
A few weeks later when he returned to the post
in a panic because the drugs weren't working, the most

the doctors could do for him was double the dose.
He was disciplined by his battalion after he ran-
sacked a house, but only because it belonged to a man
who was well-connected. He was disciplined again
when he flipped out on patrol. Someone fired a gun
at his squad from a nearby farm and he sent
twenty grenades into the house then he went
storming in, cornered the farmer and his two
dogs, demanded, "Where the hell is the shooter?"
(There was an AK shell-casing on the ground.)
The man didn't answer. He shot one of the hounds.
He asked him again. When the man said I don't know,
he shot the other one. The Lieutenant said, "Go
cool off in the truck." Outside, a herd of goats
were grazing. He levelled them all with his M-240,
ordered a private to shoot the two cows, quickly
went back, and without the slightest twinge of remorse,
shot and killed the farmer's only horse.

He was put on report, but there wasn't much they could do.
And some of the others had started losing it too.
In May, while Bastien was home on leave, he got thrown
in jail for beating his wife. The first week in June
Bressler's best friend was killed in a firefight.
For a while, when he talked about it, he seemed all right.
He'd always been a friendly guy, stable
and mellow, a regular at the poker table.
But now he began to withdraw. In July, he attacked
his commanding officer, threatening to hack
him to bits.
                    Eastridge went on one more mission.
He was manning a Humvee's M-240 machine gun,
guarding the street while the rest of his platoon
went into a house. He told the CO he was going
to bag him some hadjis. The Lieutenant thought he was joking,
but as soon as the officer left, he started shooting.
Families were out playing soccer and barbecuing.
He poured a long burst into a colonnade

of palms where a few old men stood in the shade.
Everyone started running. They piled in cars
and sped away. Eastridge put his cross hairs
on every one that moved. Car Bombs, Car Bombs
were all he could think of and he just went on
firing. Orders came over the intercom
to cease and desist, but he kept yelling, "Negative!
Negative!"
At the court martial, he was given
extra guard duty for nine counts: possession
of illegal drugs, disobeying an order, and so on.
But murdering civilians wasn't one of them.
When friends asked how many he had killed, he was un-
flappable: "Not that many, maybe a dozen."

In August they found four hundred and sixty-three
unprescribed Valium pills stashed in his laundry
and a naked female soldier in his bed.
When confronted he screamed he'd suck the blood
out of the Sergeant and spit it at his kid.
It wasn't his numerous war crimes, but sex and drugs
that got him sent to prison camp for a month.
He got a health screening as part of the court-martial
and was diagnosed with depression, anti-social
personality, hearing loss, anxiety
and chronic PTSD. Commanders decided
that he was too dangerous to stay in Iraq.
In September, 2007, the Army sent him back
to Colorado Springs, out of that mayhem
into a war the warriors brought home with them.

19.

Bastien drove his silver Audi to get
some smokes, after a night's drinking, with Bressler.
He was still in town because he'd been arrested
for beating and burning his wife with cigarettes.
Bressler had been sent back from Iraq and was waiting
to be discharged for PTSD. It was late

when they spotted a private they didn't know, Robert James,
coming out of a bar. They stopped to give him a ride,
but after they had him in the car they decided
to rob him. They drove into a dark parking lot
where he gave them a few rumpled bills, but Bressler shot
him twice in the chest anyway. He never said why.

20.

In September, under escort, Eastridge would fly
back from Baghdad. When the MP's waded into the crowd
to retrieve their bags, he took a cab downtown
and holed up in a cheap hotel. He was facing
discharge without honor, and jail time for missing a court date.

The trial for domestic violence was still pending,
and the only people he knew in town were Bastien
and Bressler. He said, "When they picked me up they were acting
weird. They asked, 'Do you want to go rob a taxi?
Do you want to kill someone' I thought they were ragging
on me, but they were crazy. We started haggling.
I needed to steal some money, but I wanted to do it
alone." Unfortunately, Eastridge knew it
couldn't be done without a car and a gun.
They tried to hold up a manager as she was coming
out of her club, but they botched it then drove around
till they found a young woman, alone, ran her down,
and grabbed her bag. Bastien started to stab her.
When she tried to resist, Eastridge got out, straddled her,
pulled out a pistol and told her to stay on her back
or he'd shoot. She couldn't identify her attackers.

But the incident sobered Eastridge up. He went
to the Sheriff's office, turned himself in and spent
most of the month in the El Paso County jail.
On the 27th he was released on bail.
A few days after that he returned to Fort Carson
but an "other than honorable" discharge for possession
of drugs meant that he was no longer eligible

for health care. He was unemployed, and unemployable.
"I had no job training, no skills that were marketable,"
he said, "All I really knew how to do was kill people."

21.

A few days later Eastridge was out, downing
shots with Bastien and Bressler at Rendezvous Lounge,
The Thirsty Parrot, and after that, Rum Bay
where they met Kevin Shields, an Iraqi vet celebrating
his twenty-fourth birthday. They all bar-hopped until closing
then drove around, lost, in the west end, smoking
a joint and a fight broke out when the soldier teased
Bressler for throwing up in the car. When he needed
to upchuck again he told Bastien to pull over.
He leaned against a pole as if he were going
to puke, then turned and shot Shields in the head.
When he fell, Bressler walked over, slowly, stood
above him and shot four more times. He took
things out of the dead man's pockets to make it look
like a mugging. Then they sped away. But witnesses
told the Police they had seen the men drinking together.
Bressler and Bastien got sixty years for conspiracy
to commit murder. Eastridge got ten as accessory.

None of them offered PTSD as a defense,
but other soldiers have said what they thought made sense:
"The Army trained us to be this way. They took
regular guys, worked on them hard, shook
apart their self esteem with a situation
in which they suffered insults, humiliation
and physical provocations but couldn't fight back.
They did it to make us angry enough to attack
and kill other human beings without a pang.
Then instead of trying to change us back, they hang
us up and out to dry. It really sucks,
all that wreckage just to save a few bucks."

22.

The Army says they're trying to fix it. They
are concerned, though they still believe war works, today
as it has throughout History (unfortunately) —
"It's the only way to keep the Peace and be free."

"The first step to a solution is understanding,"
said Major General Graham who took command
at Fort Carson just before the worst
of the violence. "There are little problems first,
then the little problems grow until they explode."

More than most, he knew what it costs to make
war. He'd watched officer training break
the mind of a son who committed suicide.
Another was killed in Iraq by an IED.
Under his watch, a program designed by the Army
doubled their counselors. Soldiers who went to see
a doctor, for any malady, even a sprained
ankle or a persistent headache were screened
for depression and PTSD. In each brigade
a Master Resiliency Trainer tried to persuade
the troops that their psyches need to be toughened the same way
their bodies were by Drill Sergeants back in the day,
and a special unit was created to track
those who were too traumatized to remain in Iraq.

But the new programs did not work as well
as expected. After two years, violent outbreaks were still
common. One of the Lethal Warriors killed
a nineteen year old girlfriend. Another shot
a pregnant woman dead. A third was brought
to trial for breaking a civilian's jaw
and dozens of others had run-ins with the law.

Jose Barco, burned so badly he still has trouble sweating,
was arrested on suspicion of domestic
battery. His second offence was drunk driving.

Then burglary with a deadly weapon. His wife
divorced him. He got into an argument
at a drunken party, pulled out a pistol and sent
three rounds into the ceiling. There was a fight.
He was thrown out and drove off into the night.
A few minutes later he was back, spraying
bullets at the crowd on the lawn. They
dispersed but Ginny Stefánic was hit in the thigh
and Barco's out on bail, awaiting trial.

Jomar Falu-Vives started hitting his wife.
The Army brat seemed able to handle life
in the combat zone without any problems, but
he turned mean when he got home. One night he stuck
a forty-five in his wife's mouth. She called
Fort Carson, asked them for help before he killed
someone. Politely, very politely, they stalled
as they had with Marquez. In May, Falu-Vives was riding
in the back of Rodolfo Torres-Gandarilla's Chrysler,
on their way home from a bar. Near South Circle Drive
he saw two men standing in front of a house on the corner.
He lifted his AK without a word of warning,
aimed calmly and fired off four rounds
knocking Captain Zachary Szody to the ground
with a bullet in his hip and one in his knee.

Ten days later, cruising in his black Chevy
Tahoe with Rodolfo and two Army buddies,
He shouted, "Give me the gun!" He shot Amairany
Cervantes, and her boyfriend, repeatedly
in the back. Both of them were killed instantly.
He sped back home and stood on the balcony,
watching, as red and blue lights converged around
the crime scene, sirens wailing. He held up his hands,
according to witnesses, and said, "I love that sound."

23.

John Needham tried to kill himself in Iraq.
He'd been hit by six roadside bombs before he cracked.
At Walter Reed, they put him on anti-psychotics,
anti-depressants, a cocktail of other narcotics,
and a powerful blood pressure drug to control his nightmares.
But there were side effects. He'd sleepwalk down stairs,
hallucinated, had unpredictable flare-ups,
short term memory loss and panic attacks.
His commanders wanted to send him back to Iraq
but his father and an Army friend intervened.
Then the Sergeants started to really lean on him.
They wrote stuff on the barracks chalkboard: We know you:
Johnny Needham, shit bag, whiny bitch boohoo.

He was paranoid and afraid of crowds. Often
he'd hide out, drink himself all the way to oblivion.
It took eight months before he was finally
discharged, honorably, with PTSD.
But he was severely changed. One night, late,
his father found him in the bathroom, naked,
smearing himself with cosmetics as camouflage paint.
He'd sharpen one end of a broomstick to make a weapon
and crouch behind the couch. He begged for a gun
but they compromised on a toy pistol. The treatment
he was getting from VA wasn't enough. He needed
to be committed, but all the beds were filled.

On September first he and his girlfriend were chilling
out in his bedroom. His father was showering upstairs.
A former flame came by and the women went hairy,
scratching and kicking and screaming. The only thing
his father heard was the Police breaking in.
They found the former girlfriend's body, dead
on the bed, and Needham naked, covered with blood.

In May, Thomas Wooly, the soldier Needham replaced
as a Humvee turret gunner in Bahgdad that day
a thousand years ago, was drinking with friends
at a party a few blocks away from Fort Carson when
a jealous husband banged on the door. Wooly
flashed back to combat mode, cocked a fully
loaded pistol and would have shot, but the man
went away. He drunkenly tried to release the hammer.
It slipped and he killed Lisa Baumann who was standing
on the other side of the room. He is charged with manslaughter.
His grandmother, Gladys, who was serving two blocks away
from him in Iraq, said, "He a good boy, but they
blowed him up so much his brains is gone which-a-way."

Then two weeks later, Roy Mason, twenty-eight,
went AWOL, sat on the beach, made a call straight
to Security, asking them, please, to clean up the mess
before the kids came down the next day. He confessed
to war crimes he saw and committed in combat, then put
the forty-five caliber Colt in his mouth and shot.

The director of a private clinic that treats
Fort Carson soldiers has warned that repeated
deployments raise the level of combat stress
and create problems counselling can't correct
by merely dealing with symptoms. "What we need
is less trauma." Major General Graham agreed,
but he said, "The Army has a job to do
and deployments are not expected to slow."

The same day Mason shot himself and bled out on the sand,
The Lethal Warriors were re-deployed to Afghanistan.

FREELANCE

A tight cloud
inches across the blue
desert like a fist

and I recognize the density
of isolation, a mirror
of what it feels like

to travel through this war
-torn country without
a language to steer by.

Late sun flares
from a window
like the last flash

of a sword before the fury
of some ancient battlefield
closed for the day. History

doesn't change, here
or anywhere. It's like
water that travels forever

but stays the same
river, under the sun's bright shield
under the moon's blade.

BIG PICTURE

It keeps changing, but only because what we're told
is what they're told to tell us, those who read the cards
and tiptoe in their crisp suits across the abyss of everyday air
waves, like oracles looking over our heads, at the words
projected *ex cathedra* through cyberspace
by the invisible ones who know their history
is a curtain call, further and further away
from the stage, like our understanding of the dead
languages we can still read but that have no echoes.

~

It's true, though we hate to admit it.
Market Forces are totally helpless
against bad weather. Tsunamis
rise up and gallop over the coastline.
Volcanos blow their tops. The earth
itself quakes and shudders under mud
-slide and rock-fall in punishing rain.

But if we took those MF's firmly in hand
they might be able to do something
about the air that makes it necessary
to put vending machines on the streets
where citizens can attempt to prevent
asphyxia by renting a couple of minutes
mouth to mouth with an oxygen mask;
or about lakes that have become so
clear, all the way down to schist
and sand, you can see the absolute
nothing that's left inside them,
unthinkable, and such a startling
blue, like Sani-Flush in a toilet.

~

We've come to consensus — too much Democracy interferes
with the purity of Warfare. And no one seems to remember
how the stones came back to live in the fields, in the river,
after the battlements fell into disrepair
and the long campaigns came home to curl up and rest
in paper scrolls. It's not so much that the past
is repeating itself, it's that we keep telling the same tales
taller, about progress and sacrifice and civilization
and of course heroes who can save anything,
even daylight, or freedom, and will keep everything
just as it is right now, forever.

~

It is terrible to be chosen, by Him, by Destiny.
Sooner or later you will have to kill,
or be killed by, those who were also told
they would inherit what's left of the Earth, after
the prophecies have been fulfilled.

~

Pre-emptive. Shock and Awe. Full Spectrum Dominance. The Axis
of Evil pokes up out of the ground right in the middle
of a Presidential Briefing in the Rose Garden. It looks like
a May Pole, or a drive shaft connecting big wheeled Capital
movers and heads of state who listen only to God.

~

Fire-bursts and blood-smoke, nearly unrecognizable
body parts in the cratered streets, and flies,
lots of flies that rise up in sizzling clouds
when the starved dog packs arrive, tear apart
the calf with no front legs, the singed chickens,
then sniff at a small boy and his sister, curled up
in a doorway with neat holes in their skulls.

~

The dead return to us in a dream.
They are intense, enlightened. Their eyes
have the transparency of sunlit flame
but when we hear what they've come to say
we know it's already too late.

DEPOSITION: THE NEW WORLD ORDER

On the day in question
the sky grew dark with storm clouds early
in the afternoon. Fires broke out
all over the city. The wind came up and ripped
leaves from the trees, pennants
from their strings above car dealerships.
In the Parks, on the grounds of the Legislature,
hailstones pummeled the blowing flower heads.

Then pinwheels of white light came down through the clouds
and cut across the countryside, churning
deep ruts that drained our lakes
and reservoirs to a network of ditches.

We were, as you can imagine, puzzled and not
a little concerned. We wanted to know
what was happening and we became suspicious
when the authorities said it was all within
normal parameters for this region, for this time
of the year. We took to the streets, but they
insisted. It was only natural and it would pass.

Our numbers grew.
We marched on the Capitol.
The police lobbed canisters of tear gas into the crowds,
used their batons with reckless abandon, arrested
as many as they could squeeze into their armored vans.
We did not *want* violence, but some of us grew tired
of the beatings, the insults, the badges, the clubs, the guns,
and instead of turning the other cheek,
we swarmed the boys and girls in blue, neutralized
their weapons and drove them back. A few minutes later,
a shotgun blast exploded a store window
& all hell broke loose.

After that we decided to become more or less
invisible, but things kept happening —
night birds flying blind in the light of day, arthritic
trees creased and scarred from their dances with lightning,
prayer shawls, worry beads, chasubles and altar linens
draped over the fenceposts of abandoned yards
and gardens.

We have no idea what it means,
if whatever got broken can be fixed,
or what sort of world we'll have to live in
now that the air is charged with particles
that burn in green drifts after dark.

NOTES

"Simulacrum"

The title is intended to refer to the work of Jean Baudrillard. The following text is particularly relevant: *Jean Baudrillard, Selected Writings*, ed. Mark Poster (Stanford; Stanford University Press, 1988). See, especially, pp. 164-188.

"Twilight/Daylight"

A single cluster bomb contains hundreds of bomblets which are scattered over what is called its footprint, an area as large as two or three football fields. With a dud rate of from 5 to 23 per cent, thousands of UXO's (unexploded ordnance) remain lethal for decades and pose a severe threat to civilians both during and after an attack. UN experts have estimated that there are as many as one million of these submunitions in Lebanon as a result of the 2006 Israel-Lebanon conflict. In addition, some bomblets, such as the BLU-97/B used in the CBU-87, are colored bright yellow to increase their visibility and warn off civilians. However, the color, coupled with their small and nonthreatening appearance, has caused children to interpret them as toys.

"Freedom's Front Line"

This poem is based on the stories recorded by Vietnam Veterans during a treatment program run by Dr. H. W. Chalsma and published in his book, *The Chambers of Memory:* PTSD *in the Life Stories of U. S. Vietnam Veterans* (Jason Aronson Inc., Publishers; Northvale, NJ and London, England, 1998). The second epigraph is from *Achilles in Vietnam: Combat Trauma and the Undoing of Character,* by Johathan Shay M. D., PH. D. (Scribner, New York, 1994, 2003)

"Lethal Warriors"

The men referred to in this poem served in a single 500-soldier unit within the 2nd Battalion, 12th Infantry Regiment of the 4th Infantry Division's 4th Brigade, a Combat Team which nicknamed itself "The Lethal Warriors." Since returning to the US in 2006, ten members have been arrested for murder, attempted murder or manslaughter. Others have either committed suicide or attempted to do so. The homicide rate for this regiment was a hundred and fourteen times higher than the rate for civilian Colorado Springs. Since 2005, the Brigade's returning soldiers have been involved in brawls, beatings, rapes, DUI's, drug deals, domestic violence, shootings, stabbings, kidnappings and suicides.

It should also be noted that only a small percentage of all those who served in the Armed Forces behaved in this way when they returned home. But because of the Stop Loss policy, many who engaged in combat had done two or three, and in the severest cases of PTSD, even four tours of up to fifteen months each, much longer than in Vietnam, where soldiers were normally rotated home after a year. Among those who experienced heavy combat, the percentage who committed crimes at home is alarmingly high.

See "Casualties of War, The Hell of War Comes Home" by David Phillips, *The Colorado Springs Gazette,* Part I, July 25 and Part II, July 28, 2009. Material from these articles was collated with information from the following sources:

Chris Hedges and Laila Al-Arian, *Collateral Damage* (Nation Books, New York, 2008)

Dahr Jamail, *The Will to Resist,* (Haymarket Books, Chicago, 2009)

Camilo Mejia, *Road from ar Ramadi,* (Haymarket Books, Chicago, 2008)

"Deposition: The New World Order"
One of the meanings of "Deposition" is "a work of art depicting Christ being lowered from the cross" (paintings by Carravagio, Raphael, and Michelangelo's Florence Pietá, for example), hence the afternoon darkness in the opening lines.

ABOUT THE AUTHOR

George Amabile has published his poetry, fiction and non-fiction in the USA, Canada, Europe, England, Wales, South America, Australia and New Zealand in over a hundred anthologies, magazines, journals and periodicals including *The New Yorker, The New Yorker Book of Poems, Harper's, Poetry (Chicago), American Poetry Review, Botteghe Oscure, The Globe and Mail, The Malahat Review, The Penguin Book of Canadian Verse, Saturday Night,, Poetry Australia, Sur (Buenos Aires), Poetry Canada Review, and Canadian Literature.*

Amabile has published ten books. *The Presence of Fire* won the CAA National Prize for literature; his long poem, *Durée,* placed third in the CBC Literary Competition (1991); "What We Take with Us, Going Away" was shortlisted for the CBC Literary Prize (2003) and he is the subject of a special issue of *Prairie Fire*, (Vol. 21, No. 1, May 2000). "Diminuendo" was awarded third prize in the Petra Kenney International Poetry Competition (2005); "A Raft of Lilies" won second place in the MWG national poetry contest (2007); "Snow Birds, with Twelve Pelicans" took second place and "Design, after Herakleitos" won first prize in the *Writers' Digest* International Rhymed Poetry Contest (2013, 2014). His most recent publications are *Small Change* (Fiction, Libros Libertad, 2011) and a long poem, *Dancing, with Mirrors (*Porcupine's Quill, 2011), both of which won Bressani awards.

Eco-Audit

Printing this book using Rolland Enviro Print 100 instead of virgin-fibre paper saved the following resources:

Trees	Solid Waste	Water	Air Emissions
2	67 kg	5,494 L	221 kg